HAPPINESS
DIARY

THE 180 DAY CHALLENGE
TO A HAPPIER WAY OF LIFE

Narissa Phipps

The Book Guild Ltd

First published in Great Britain in 2016 by
The Book Guild Ltd
9 Priory Business Park
Wistow Road, Kibworth
Leicestershire, LE8 0RX
Freephone: 0800 999 2982
www.bookguild.co.uk
Email: info@bookguild.co.uk
Twitter: @bookguild

Typeset in Centaur MT

Printed and bound by CPI Group (UK) Ltd, Croydon, CR0 4YY

ISBN 978 1 911 3200 81

British Library Cataloguing in Publication Data.
A catalogue record for this book is available from the British Library.

For my Dad

My best friend, favourite teacher and inspiration.
Always supporting, encouraging and believing.
Forever in my heart.

HELLO!

Welcome to your very own Happiness Diary, congratulations on completing the first step on your path to a more positive way of life. If you have bravely purchased this without much knowledge of its content or have received it as a kind gift the following paragraphs will be particularly beneficial for you to read. You are now part of a network of people who have embarked on a journey for 180 days dedicated to shifting the brains negativity bias to a more positive one. Each page is designed so that even just a quick five minutes of writing a day has the potential to have a huge impact. However like anything the more you are willing to put in the more likely you are to reap the benefits. I therefore invite you to be as creative as you dare and to help inspire others. If you ever need a boost of motivation or want to share one of your challenge experiences, we would love to hear from you via our Facebook page.

You will notice in the top corner there is a blank date space for you to fill in. This is so that you have some guilt free flexibility on those days where it is just not possible to complete. Although please note that the days where you feel that you do not have the time may be the ones where it is most beneficial to make the time. To start each day you will give it purpose by setting three goals that you will strive to complete before it comes to an end. You will then read your daily contemplation and be met with your challenge. It is perfectly okay to swap the challenge if you find that is not practical for you to do on that day. However please bear in mind that a challenge is designed to be just that, the ideas were produced to be easily be integrated into your day therefore be cautious that you are not simply avoiding a certain task. If you do find yourself wanting to avoid one, do it as soon as possible. Trust me, the time you spend prancing outside the cold shower testing a toe does not make it any warmer! Once you have completed your daily challenge make note of this however you wish, perhaps with a tick or by colouring the cloud in. You could also highlight which ones you particularly liked so that you can benefit from making your own challenges to do them again. When the day draws to a close you will reflect on its events by showing gratitude, being kind to yourself, focusing on your favourite moment and finally by welcoming tomorrow. There is a blank page after every 30 days, please feel free to use these for your own reflection and headspace.

Throughout the diary there are six main themes based on the current research of how to increase happiness. I categorise these as mindfulness, exercising, trying, socialising, nurturing and giving. Some of you may already be practising mindfulness whilst others may have never heard of it before. There is a lot of good literature already available on the subject and I see no benefit to repeat it here so if you are unsure then please use your chosen search engine and video sharing website to find out more.

The challenges have been designed to be suitable for the average person. As this now belongs to you please make it your own, tailor it to your life. For example if you already regularly do the stated challenge you will need to make some modifications for it to be stimulating. Similarly if you have just had major surgery, please do not read '20 minute jog' and feel you have to evacuate your hospital bed and do laps of the ward. Know your limits and adapt your diary to you, consulting your physician if you need to. Some quick ideas are changing the frequency, duration, intensity, location, intention, mindset and belief. For example your 20 minutes of exercise could be spent cleaning, believing this is exercise, thinking about the muscles you are stretching, the calories you are burning and the better sleep you will have later. I encourage you to use your imagination at every opportunity. Please do not feel that you need a large bank balance to complete the challenges. Something new can be as simple and cheap as a bus ticket or a different style of tea if that is all your budget allows. Just remember that whatever you do spend is an investment in your happiness. If you ever get a creative block and would like some new ideas the network is here for you via the Facebook page.

I have obtained all the contemplations throughout the diary either from my own thoughts or sources that I deem to be reliable. I have shared my findings with the best intentions of accuracy, however if there are any discrepancies I do sincerely apologise. For anyone who would like to visit these websites or find out more please find the links below.

www.actionforhappiness.org

www.bemindful.co.uk

www.brainyquote.com

www.freemindfulness.org

www.mind.org.uk

www.ngkids.co.uk

www.nhs.uk/livewell

www.oxfordmindfulness.org

www.projecthappiness.org

www.ted.com

BEGIN!

I now pass the writing over to you so enjoy your Happiness Diary and all the experiences you will have because of it. Whatever happens, always remember to keep smiling!

Before the day comes to an end I wish to have achieved:

1. --

2. --

3. --

CONTEMPLATE TODAY:

BODIES GIVE OFF A TINY AMOUNT OF LIGHT THAT IS TOO WEAK FOR THE EYES TO SEE

CHALLENGE TOMORROW:

BRIGHTEN UP SOMEONE'S DAY

Three things I am thankful for today are:

1. --

2. --

3. --

Today I am proud of myself for:

My favourite moment of today was:

Tomorrow I am looking forward to:

DATE . ./. ./. .

Before the day comes to an end I wish to have achieved:

1. --

2. --

3. --

CONTEMPLATE TODAY:

PHYSICAL ACTIVITY CAN GET YOU GOING WHEN
YOU ARE IMMOBILISED – JOHN DAVIDSON

CHALLENGE TOMORROW:

WHEN YOU FEEL LETHARGIC, TAKE A
TEN-MINUTE BREAK TO EXERCISE

Three things I am thankful for today are:

1. --

2. --

3. --

Today I am proud of myself for:

My favourite moment of today was:

Tomorrow I am looking forward to:

Before the day comes to an end I wish to have achieved:

1. --

2. --

3. --

CONTEMPLATE TODAY:

WHEN YOU LEARN, YOU CHANGE THE STRUCTURE OF YOUR BRAIN

CHALLENGE TOMORROW:

WATCH A DOCUMENTARY ON A SUBJECT THAT REALLY INTERESTS YOU

Three things I am thankful for today are:

1. --

2. --

3. --

Today I am proud of myself for:

My favourite moment of today was:

Tomorrow I am looking forward to:

DATE . ./. ./. .

Before the day comes to an end I wish to have achieved:

1. ---

2. ---

3. ---

Three things I am thankful for today are:

1. ---

2. ---

3. ---

Today I am proud of myself for:

My favourite moment of today was:

Tomorrow I am looking forward to:

Before the day comes to an end I wish to have achieved:

1. ---

2. ---

3. ---

CONTEMPLATE TODAY:

MINDFULNESS IS THE PRACTICE OF BEING AWARE OF YOUR BODY, MIND AND FEELINGS IN THE PRESENT MOMENT

CHALLENGE TOMORROW:

RESEARCH MINDFULNESS TO TEACH YOURSELF MORE ABOUT IT

Three things I am thankful for today are:

1. ---

2. ---

3. ---

Today I am proud of myself for:

My favourite moment of today was:

Tomorrow I am looking forward to:

DATE . ./. ./. .

Before the day comes to an end I wish to have achieved:

1. --

2. --

3. --

CONTEMPLATE TODAY:

OUR DOUBTS ARE TRAITORS AND MAKE US LOSE THE GOOD
WE OFT MIGHT WIN BY FEARING TO ATTEMPT – WILLIAM SHAKESPEARE

CHALLENGE TOMORROW:

DO SOMETHING THAT SCARES YOU

Three things I am thankful for today are:

1. --

2. --

3. --

Today I am proud of myself for:

My favourite moment of today was:

Tomorrow I am looking forward to:

Before the day comes to an end I wish to have achieved:

1. --

2. --

3. --

CONTEMPLATE TODAY:

THE BEST WAY TO CHEER YOURSELF UP IS TO TRY TO CHEER SOMEBODY ELSE UP – MARK TWAIN

CHALLENGE TOMORROW:

SURPRISE SOMEONE YOU LOVE

Three things I am thankful for today are:

1. --

2. --

3. --

Today I am proud of myself for:

My favourite moment of today was:

Tomorrow I am looking forward to:

DATE . ./. ./. .

Before the day comes to an end I wish to have achieved:

1. ....

2. ....

3. ....

CONTEMPLATE TODAY:

RESEARCH SHOWS THAT EXERCISE CAN BOOST ENERGY

CHALLENGE TOMORROW:
START THE DAY WITH A QUICK 15-MINUTE BURST OF EXERCISE

Three things I am thankful for today are:

1. ....

2. ....

3. ....

Today I am proud of myself for:

....

My favourite moment of today was:

....

Tomorrow I am looking forward to:

....

Before the day comes to an end I wish to have achieved:

1. --

2. --

3. --

CONTEMPLATE TODAY:

THE JOURNEY OF A THOUSAND MILES
BEGINS WITH ONE STEP — LAO TZU

CHALLENGE TOMORROW:
SET A CHALLENGING GOAL AND A DATE TO ACHIEVE.
LOOK AT IT DAILY UNTIL YOU DO IT

Three things I am thankful for today are:

1. --

2. --

3. --

Today I am proud of myself for:

My favourite moment of today was:

Tomorrow I am looking forward to:

DATE . ./. ./. .

Before the day comes to an end I wish to have achieved:

1. --

2. --

3. --

CONTEMPLATE TODAY:

HOW GRATEFUL ARE YOU?

CHALLENGE TOMORROW:
VISIT WWW.TED.COM AND WATCH LOUIE SCHWARTZBERG'S
TALK ON NATURE, BEAUTY AND GRATITUDE

Three things I am thankful for today are:

1. --

2. --

3. --

Today I am proud of myself for:

My favourite moment of today was:

Tomorrow I am looking forward to:

Before the day comes to an end I wish to have achieved:

1. ---

2. ---

3. ---

CONTEMPLATE TODAY:

SO THE DARKNESS SHALL BE THE LIGHT AND THE
STILLNESS THE DANCING — T. S. ELIOT

CHALLENGE TOMORROW:

VISIT WWW.TED.COM AND WATCH PICO
IYER'S TALK ON STILLNESS

Three things I am thankful for today are:

1. ---

2. ---

3. ---

Today I am proud of myself for:

My favourite moment of today was:

Tomorrow I am looking forward to:

DATE . ./. ./. .

Before the day comes to an end I wish to have achieved:

1. ....

2. ....

3. ....

CONTEMPLATE TODAY:

THERE IS ALWAYS TIME TO
EXPERIENCE NEW THINGS

CHALLENGE TOMORROW:

BE BOLD AND CHOOSE TO DO
SOMETHING DIFFERENTLY

Three things I am thankful for today are:

1. ....

2. ....

3. ....

Today I am proud of myself for:

....

My favourite moment of today was:

....

Tomorrow I am looking forward to:

....

Before the day comes to an end I wish to have achieved:

1. --

2. --

3. --

CONTEMPLATE TODAY:

WHO DO YOU FIND IT REALLY DIFFICULT
TO HAVE WARM FEELINGS TOWARDS?

CHALLENGE TOMORROW:
DO SOMETHING NICE FOR THE ABOVE PERSON,
ANONYMOUSLY IF YOU WISH

Three things I am thankful for today are:

1. --

2. --

3. --

Today I am proud of myself for:

My favourite moment of today was:

Tomorrow I am looking forward to:

DATE . ./. ./. .

Before the day comes to an end I wish to have achieved:

1. --

2. --

3. --

CONTEMPLATE TODAY:

JUST 10 MINUTES OF BRISK WALKING INCREASES OUR
MENTAL ALERTNESS, ENERGY AND POSITIVE MOOD

CHALLENGE TOMORROW:

DO A 10-MINUTE POWER WALK

Three things I am thankful for today are:

1. --

2. --

3. --

Today I am proud of myself for:

My favourite moment of today was:

Tomorrow I am looking forward to:

Before the day comes to an end I wish to have achieved:

1. --

2. --

3. --

CONTEMPLATE TODAY:

WHAT DO YOU REALLY LOVE TO DO?

CHALLENGE TOMORROW:

WRITE YOUR ANSWERS TO THE ABOVE HERE:

Three things I am thankful for today are:

1. --

2. --

3. --

Today I am proud of myself for:

My favourite moment of today was:

Tomorrow I am looking forward to:

DATE . ./. ./. .

Before the day comes to an end I wish to have achieved:

1. ---

2. ---

3. ---

CONTEMPLATE TODAY:

HAVING STRONG SOCIAL SUPPORT CAN INCREASE
OUR IMMUNITY TO INFECTION

CHALLENGE TOMORROW:

CONTACT SOMEONE YOU HAVE NOT
SPOKEN TO IN A WHILE

Three things I am thankful for today are:

1. ---

2. ---

3. ---

Today I am proud of myself for:

My favourite moment of today was:

Tomorrow I am looking forward to:

Before the day comes to an end I wish to have achieved:

1. --

2. --

3. --

CONTEMPLATE TODAY:

THERE ARE MANY DIFFERENT WAYS TO PRACTICE MINDFULNESS

CHALLENGE TOMORROW:

RESEARCH THEM, WRITE DOWN WHAT YOU WOULD LIKE TO TRY

Three things I am thankful for today are:

1. --

2. --

3. --

Today I am proud of myself for:

My favourite moment of today was:

Tomorrow I am looking forward to:

DATE . ./. ./. .

Before the day comes to an end I wish to have achieved:

1. --

2. --

3. --

CONTEMPLATE TODAY:

Approximately 70% of the Earth's surface is water

CHALLENGE TOMORROW:

Make water the only liquid you drink

Three things I am thankful for today are:

1. --

2. --

3. --

Today I am proud of myself for:

My favourite moment of today was:

Tomorrow I am looking forward to:

Before the day comes to an end I wish to have achieved:

1. --

2. --

3. --

CONTEMPLATE TODAY:

NO ONE HAS EVER BECOME POOR BY GIVING
– ANNE FRANK

CHALLENGE TOMORROW:
THINK OF SOMEONE WHO WOULD BENEFIT FROM THIS
DIARY, BUY IT FOR THEM, ANONYMOUSLY
IF YOU CAN

Three things I am thankful for today are:

1. --

2. --

3. --

Today I am proud of myself for:

My favourite moment of today was:

Tomorrow I am looking forward to:

DATE . ./. ./. .

Before the day comes to an end I wish to have achieved:

1. ---

2. ---

3. ---

CONTEMPLATE TODAY:
EXERCISE MAKES YOU SMARTER. FOR A
PERIOD OF TIME AFTER YOU EXERCISE A CHEMICAL IS
PRODUCED THAT MAKES YOUR BRAIN MORE WILLING TO LEARN

CHALLENGE TOMORROW:
EXERCISE FOR 20 MINUTES

Three things I am thankful for today are:

1. ---

2. ---

3. ---

Today I am proud of myself for:

My favourite moment of today was:

Tomorrow I am looking forward to:

Before the day comes to an end I wish to have achieved:

1. --

2. --

3. --

CONTEMPLATE TODAY:

LIFE IS NOT A MATTER OF MILESTONES
BUT OF MOMENTS – ROSE KENNEDY

CHALLENGE TOMORROW:

TAKE A PICTURE OF SOMETHING
THAT MAKES YOU SMILE

Three things I am thankful for today are:

1. --

2. --

3. --

Today I am proud of myself for:

My favourite moment of today was:

Tomorrow I am looking forward to:

DATE . ./. ./. .

Before the day comes to an end I wish to have achieved:

1. ---

2. ---

3. ---

CONTEMPLATE TODAY:

THE MOST INFLUENTIAL EXTERNAL FACTORS AFFECTING
INDIVIDUAL HAPPINESS ARE HUMAN RELATIONSHIPS

CHALLENGE TOMORROW:
SHOW YOUR APPRECIATION TO AS MANY FAMILY
AND FRIENDS AS YOU CAN

Three things I am thankful for today are:

1. ---

2. ---

3. ---

Today I am proud of myself for:

My favourite moment of today was:

Tomorrow I am looking forward to:

Before the day comes to an end I wish to have achieved:

1. --

2. --

3. --

CONTEMPLATE TODAY:

WE TEND TO THINK OF MEDITATION IN ONLY ONE
WAY. BUT LIFE ITSELF IS A MEDITATION – RAUL JULIA

CHALLENGE TOMORROW:
GO BACK TO YOUR MINDFULNESS RESEARCH,
TRY ONE OF THE MEDITATIONS YOU FOUND

Three things I am thankful for today are:

1. --

2. --

3. --

Today I am proud of myself for:

My favourite moment of today was:

Tomorrow I am looking forward to:

DATE . ./. ./. .

Before the day comes to an end I wish to have achieved:

1. --

2. --

3. --

CONTEMPLATE TODAY:

AND THOSE WHO WERE SEEN DANCING WERE THOUGHT TO BE INSANE
BY THOSE WHO COULD NOT HEAR THE MUSIC – FRIEDRICH NIETZSCHE

CHALLENGE TOMORROW:
PLAY YOUR FAVOURITE SONG,
LET LOOSE AND DANCE

Three things I am thankful for today are:

1. --

2. --

3. --

Today I am proud of myself for:

My favourite moment of today was:

Tomorrow I am looking forward to:

Before the day comes to an end I wish to have achieved:

1. --

2. --

3. --

CONTEMPLATE TODAY:

GIVING TO OTHERS ACTIVATES THE BRAIN AREAS
ASSOCIATED WITH PLEASURE, SOCIAL CONNECTION AND TRUST

CHALLENGE TOMORROW:
THINK OF THREE PEOPLE YOU WOULD LIKE TO
GIVE A SMALL GIFT TO AND DO IT

Three things I am thankful for today are:

1. --

2. --

3. --

Today I am proud of myself for:

My favourite moment of today was:

Tomorrow I am looking forward to:

DATE . ./. ./. .

Before the day comes to an end I wish to have achieved:

1. --

2. --

3. --

CONTEMPLATE TODAY:

EXERCISE SHOULD BE REGARDED AS TRIBUTE
TO THE HEART – GENE TUNNEY

CHALLENGE TOMORROW:

DO 30 MINUTES OF EXERCISE

Three things I am thankful for today are:

1. --

2. --

3. --

Today I am proud of myself for:

My favourite moment of today was:

Tomorrow I am looking forward to:

Before the day comes to an end I wish to have achieved:

1. --

2. --

3. --

CONTEMPLATE TODAY:

HOW CAN YOU HELP YOURSELF?

CHALLENGE TOMORROW:

WRITE YOUR ANSWERS TO THE ABOVE HERE:

Three things I am thankful for today are:

1. --

2. --

3. --

Today I am proud of myself for:

My favourite moment of today was:

Tomorrow I am looking forward to:

DATE . ./. ./. .

Before the day comes to an end I wish to have achieved:

1. ....

2. ....

3. ....

CONTEMPLATE TODAY:

LOST TIME IS NEVER FOUND AGAIN
– BENJAMIN FRANKLIN

CHALLENGE TOMORROW:

ARRANGE TO CATCH UP WITH SOMEONE
YOU HAVE NOT SEEN FOR AGES

Three things I am thankful for today are:

1. ....

2. ....

3. ....

Today I am proud of myself for:

....

My favourite moment of today was:

....

Tomorrow I am looking forward to:

....

Before the day comes to an end I wish to have achieved:

1. --

2. --

3. --

CONTEMPLATE TODAY:

MINDFULNESS HAS BEEN BENEFITING PEOPLE FOR THOUSANDS OF YEARS

CHALLENGE TOMORROW:

CHOOSE ONE OF YOUR DAILY ACTIVITIES TO DO MINDFULLY

Three things I am thankful for today are:

1. --

2. --

3. --

Today I am proud of myself for:

My favourite moment of today was:

Tomorrow I am looking forward to:

DATE . ./. ./. .

Before the day comes to an end I wish to have achieved:

1. --

2. --

3. --

CONTEMPLATE TODAY:

APPROXIMATELY 70% OF THE AIR WE BREATHE IS PRODUCED BY THE OCEANS

CHALLENGE TOMORROW:

DO NOT CONSUME SEAFOOD

Three things I am thankful for today are:

1. --

2. --

3. --

Today I am proud of myself for:

My favourite moment of today was:

Tomorrow I am looking forward to:

Well Done!

Well done on completing the first 30 days of your challenge. Quite often the first part is the hardest so great work on persevering. I admire your determination and commitment. If reflection does not come easy to you, here are a few questions to help get you started. Look at your first and last dates, how many days did it take you? How do you feel now in comparison to the start? What was your favourite part? What benefits have you noticed? Which challenges would you like to keep doing? How could you improve your next 30 days?

REFLECTION

Before the day comes to an end I wish to have achieved:

1. --

2. --

3. --

CONTEMPLATE TODAY:

KIND WORDS CAN BE SHORT AND EASY TO SPEAK BUT THEIR ECHOES ARE TRULY ENDLESS – MOTHER TERESA

CHALLENGE TOMORROW:

SAY SOMETHING NICE TO THREE PEOPLE

Three things I am thankful for today are:

1. --

2. --

3. --

Today I am proud of myself for:

My favourite moment of today was:

Tomorrow I am looking forward to:

DATE . ./. ./. .

Before the day comes to an end I wish to have achieved:

1. --

2. --

3. --

CONTEMPLATE TODAY:
OUR BODIES HAVE EVOLVED TO MOVE, YET WE NOW USE
THE ENERGY IN OIL INSTEAD OF MUSCLES TO DO OUR WORK
– DAVID SUZUKI

CHALLENGE TOMORROW:
USE YOUR MUSCLES INSTEAD OF OIL
WHERE POSSIBLE

Three things I am thankful for today are:

1. --

2. --

3. --

Today I am proud of myself for:

My favourite moment of today was:

Tomorrow I am looking forward to:

Before the day comes to an end I wish to have achieved:

1. --

2. --

3. --

CONTEMPLATE TODAY:

HAPPIER PEOPLE LIVE LONGER

CHALLENGE TOMORROW:

ARRANGE TO DO ONE OF THE THINGS THAT YOU PREVIOUSLY IDENTIFIED YOU LOVE

Three things I am thankful for today are:

1. --

2. --

3. --

Today I am proud of myself for:

My favourite moment of today was:

Tomorrow I am looking forward to:

DATE . ./. ./. .

Before the day comes to an end I wish to have achieved:

1. --

2. --

3. --

CONTEMPLATE TODAY:

IN EVERY CONCEIVABLE MANNER, THE FAMILY IS LINK
TO OUR PAST, BRIDGE TO OUR FUTURE – ALEX HALEY

CHALLENGE TOMORROW:

TELL AS MANY FAMILY MEMBERS AS YOU
CAN THAT YOU LOVE THEM

Three things I am thankful for today are:

1. --

2. --

3. --

Today I am proud of myself for:

My favourite moment of today was:

Tomorrow I am looking forward to:

Before the day comes to an end I wish to have achieved:

1. --

2. --

3. --

CONTEMPLATE TODAY:
ALL THE SUFFERING, STRESS AND ADDICTION COMES
FROM NOT REALISING YOU ALREADY ARE WHAT YOU ARE
LOOKING FOR – JON KABAT-ZINN

CHALLENGE TOMORROW:
VISIT WWW.TED.COM AND WATCH ANDY
PUDDICOMBE'S TALK ON MINDFULNESS

Three things I am thankful for today are:

1. --

2. --

3. --

Today I am proud of myself for:

My favourite moment of today was:

Tomorrow I am looking forward to:

DATE . ./. ./. .

Before the day comes to an end I wish to have achieved:

1. --

2. --

3. --

CONTEMPLATE TODAY:

Life is what happens while you are busy making other plans – John Lennon

CHALLENGE TOMORROW:

Do something spontaneous

Three things I am thankful for today are:

1. --

2. --

3. --

Today I am proud of myself for:

My favourite moment of today was:

Tomorrow I am looking forward to:

Before the day comes to an end I wish to have achieved:

1. --

2. --

3. --

CONTEMPLATE TODAY:

ALTRUISTIC BEHAVIOUR RELEASES ENDORPHINS IN THE BRAIN
AND INCREASES HAPPINESS IN THE GIVER AND RECEIVER

CHALLENGE TOMORROW:

MAKE A KIND GESTURE

Three things I am thankful for today are:

1. --

2. --

3. --

Today I am proud of myself for:

My favourite moment of today was:

Tomorrow I am looking forward to:

DATE . ./. ./. .

Before the day comes to an end I wish to have achieved:

1. --

2. --

3. --

CONTEMPLATE TODAY:
IT IS MEDICALLY PROVEN THAT PEOPLE WHO DO
REGULAR PHYSICAL ACTIVITY HAVE UP TO A
30% LOWER RISK OF DEMENTIA

CHALLENGE TOMORROW:

FIND AN EXERCISE VIDEO THAT YOU
LIKE AND DO IT

Three things I am thankful for today are:

1. --

2. --

3. --

Today I am proud of myself for:

My favourite moment of today was:

Tomorrow I am looking forward to:

Before the day comes to an end I wish to have achieved:

1. ....

2. ....

3. ....

CONTEMPLATE TODAY:

A DAY WITHOUT LAUGHTER IS A DAY WASTED
– CHARLIE CHAPLIN

CHALLENGE TOMORROW:

WATCH COMEDY

Three things I am thankful for today are:

1. ....

2. ....

3. ....

Today I am proud of myself for:

....

My favourite moment of today was:

....

Tomorrow I am looking forward to:

....

DATE . ./. ./. .

Before the day comes to an end I wish to have achieved:

1. _____

2. _____

3. _____

CONTEMPLATE TODAY:

How thankful are you?

CHALLENGE TOMORROW:
Visit www.ted.com and watch Laura
Trice's talk on saying thank you

Three things I am thankful for today are:

1. _____

2. _____

3. _____

Today I am proud of myself for:

_____

My favourite moment of today was:

_____

Tomorrow I am looking forward to:

_____

Before the day comes to an end I wish to have achieved:

1. --

2. --

3. --

CONTEMPLATE TODAY:

MINDFULNESS CAN GIVE MORE INSIGHT INTO EMOTIONS

CHALLENGE TOMORROW:

CHOOSE A DIFFERENT ONE OF YOUR DAILY ACTIVITIES TO DO MINDFULLY

Three things I am thankful for today are:

1. --

2. --

3. --

Today I am proud of myself for:

My favourite moment of today was:

Tomorrow I am looking forward to:

DATE . ./. ./. .

Before the day comes to an end I wish to have achieved:

1. ....

2. ....

3. ....

CONTEMPLATE TODAY:

A SINGLE PLASTIC BAG CAN TAKE UP TO 500 YEARS
TO FULLY DISINTEGRATE IN LANDFILL

CHALLENGE TOMORROW:

DO NOT USE A PLASTIC BAG

Three things I am thankful for today are:

1. ....

2. ....

3. ....

Today I am proud of myself for:

....

My favourite moment of today was:

....

Tomorrow I am looking forward to:

....

Before the day comes to an end I wish to have achieved:

1. --

2. --

3. --

CONTEMPLATE TODAY:

YOU CANNOT LIVE A PERFECT DAY WITHOUT DOING
SOMETHING FOR SOMEONE WHO WILL NEVER
BE ABLE TO REPAY YOU – JOHN WOODEN

CHALLENGE TOMORROW:

HELP SOMEONE IN NEED

Three things I am thankful for today are:

1. --

2. --

3. --

Today I am proud of myself for:

My favourite moment of today was:

Tomorrow I am looking forward to:

DATE . ./. ./. .

Before the day comes to an end I wish to have achieved:

1. --

2. --

3. --

CONTEMPLATE TODAY:

IT IS MEDICALLY PROVEN THAT PEOPLE WHO DO REGULAR
PHYSICAL ACTIVITY HAVE A 30% LOWER RISK OF EARLY DEATH

CHALLENGE TOMORROW:

DO 20 MINUTES OF GENTLE STRETCHING

Three things I am thankful for today are:

1. --

2. --

3. --

Today I am proud of myself for:

My favourite moment of today was:

Tomorrow I am looking forward to:

Before the day comes to an end I wish to have achieved:

1. --

2. --

3. --

CONTEMPLATE TODAY:

WE DO NOT LAUGH BECAUSE WE ARE HAPPY, WE ARE HAPPY
BECAUSE WE LAUGH – WILLIAM JAMES

CHALLENGE TOMORROW:

FIND FIVE HILARIOUS JOKES

Three things I am thankful for today are:

1. --

2. --

3. --

Today I am proud of myself for:

My favourite moment of today was:

Tomorrow I am looking forward to:

DATE . ./. ./. .

Before the day comes to an end I wish to have achieved:

1. --

2. --

3. --

CONTEMPLATE TODAY:

SPREAD LOVE EVERYWHERE YOU GO. LET NO ONE EVER
COME TO YOU WITHOUT LEAVING HAPPIER — MOTHER TERESA

CHALLENGE TOMORROW:

TALK TO A STRANGER

Three things I am thankful for today are:

1. --

2. --

3. --

Today I am proud of myself for:

My favourite moment of today was:

Tomorrow I am looking forward to:

Before the day comes to an end I wish to have achieved:

1. --

2. --

3. --

CONTEMPLATE TODAY:

MINDFULNESS MEDITATION HAS BEEN SHOWN TO
AFFECT HOW THE BRAIN WORKS AND ITS STRUCTURE

CHALLENGE TOMORROW:

DO A FIVE-MINUTE BODY SCAN

Three things I am thankful for today are:

1. --

2. --

3. --

Today I am proud of myself for:

My favourite moment of today was:

Tomorrow I am looking forward to:

DATE . ./. ./. .

Before the day comes to an end I wish to have achieved:

1. ....

2. ....

3. ....

CONTEMPLATE TODAY:

He who knows best knows how little he knows
– Thomas Jefferson

CHALLENGE TOMORROW:

Do not follow the news

Three things I am thankful for today are:

1. ....

2. ....

3. ....

Today I am proud of myself for:

....

My favourite moment of today was:

....

Tomorrow I am looking forward to:

....

Before the day comes to an end I wish to have achieved:

1. --

2. --

3. --

CONTEMPLATE TODAY:

GIVING MONEY AWAY TENDS TO MAKE PEOPLE
HAPPIER THAN SPENDING IT ON THEMSELVES

CHALLENGE TOMORROW:

MAKE A DONATION TO A PERSON
OR A CAUSE

Three things I am thankful for today are:

1. --

2. --

3. --

Today I am proud of myself for:

My favourite moment of today was:

Tomorrow I am looking forward to:

DATE . ./. ./. .

Before the day comes to an end I wish to have achieved:

1. ....

2. ....

3. ....

CONTEMPLATE TODAY:

EXERCISE IS THE CHIEF SOURCE OF IMPROVEMENT
IN OUR FACULTIES – HUGH BLAIR

CHALLENGE TOMORROW:

FIND AN EXERCISE CLASS YOU WOULD
LIKE TO ATTEND, BOOK IT

Three things I am thankful for today are:

1. ....

2. ....

3. ....

Today I am proud of myself for:
....

My favourite moment of today was:
....

Tomorrow I am looking forward to:
....

Before the day comes to an end I wish to have achieved:

1. --

2. --

3. --

CONTEMPLATE TODAY:

HAPPINESS IS CONTAGIOUS

CHALLENGE TOMORROW:

SHARE THE FIVE JOKES YOU FOUND PREVIOUSLY

Three things I am thankful for today are:

1. --

2. --

3. --

Today I am proud of myself for:

My favourite moment of today was:

Tomorrow I am looking forward to:

DATE . ./. ./. .

Before the day comes to an end I wish to have achieved:

1. --

2. --

3. --

CONTEMPLATE TODAY:

YOUR BEHAVIOUR CAN REALLY HAVE AN IMPACT ON SOMEONE'S DAY

CHALLENGE TOMORROW:

INTERACT POSITIVELY WITH EVERYONE YOU MEET

Three things I am thankful for today are:

1. --

2. --

3. --

Today I am proud of myself for:

My favourite moment of today was:

Tomorrow I am looking forward to:

Before the day comes to an end I wish to have achieved:

1. --

2. --

3. --

CONTEMPLATE TODAY:

WHAT WE ACHIEVE INWARDLY WILL
CHANGE OUTER REALITY – PLUTARCH

CHALLENGE TOMORROW:

LISTEN TO PAVAROTTI'S NESSUN DORMA
MINDFULLY

Three things I am thankful for today are:

1. --

2. --

3. --

Today I am proud of myself for:

My favourite moment of today was:

Tomorrow I am looking forward to:

DATE . ./. ./. .

Before the day comes to an end I wish to have achieved:

1. --

2. --

3. --

CONTEMPLATE TODAY:

STUDIES SHOW THAT MONEY SPENT ON TRAVELLING MAKES YOU HAPPIER THAN MATERIAL GOODS

CHALLENGE TOMORROW:

TREAT YOURSELF TO A TRIP TO SOMEWHERE YOU HAVE NEVER BEEN BEFORE

Three things I am thankful for today are:

1. --

2. --

3. --

Today I am proud of myself for:

My favourite moment of today was:

Tomorrow I am looking forward to:

Before the day comes to an end I wish to have achieved:

1. --

2. --

3. --

CONTEMPLATE TODAY:

BE KIND, FOR EVERYONE YOU MEET IS
FIGHTING A HARD BATTLE – PHILO

CHALLENGE TOMORROW:

GO OUT OF YOUR WAY TO BE TRULY NICE TO
EVERYONE YOU INTERACT WITH

Three things I am thankful for today are:

1. --

2. --

3. --

Today I am proud of myself for:

My favourite moment of today was:

Tomorrow I am looking forward to:

DATE . ./. ./. .

Before the day comes to an end I wish to have achieved:

1. --

2. --

3. --

CONTEMPLATE TODAY:

IN EVERY WALK WITH NATURE ONE RECEIVES
FAR MORE THAN HE SEEKS — JOHN MUIR

CHALLENGE TOMORROW:

GO FOR A 20-MINUTE WALK IN NATURE

Three things I am thankful for today are:

1. --

2. --

3. --

Today I am proud of myself for:

My favourite moment of today was:

Tomorrow I am looking forward to:

Before the day comes to an end I wish to have achieved:

1. --

2. --

3. --

CONTEMPLATE TODAY:

JEALOUSY IS ALL THE FUN YOU THINK THEY HAD
– ERICA JONG

CHALLENGE TOMORROW:
DO NOT LET YOUR MIND WANDER TO IMAGINARY
SCENARIOS THAT BRING YOU DOWN

Three things I am thankful for today are:

1. --

2. --

3. --

Today I am proud of myself for:

My favourite moment of today was:

Tomorrow I am looking forward to:

DATE . ./. ./. .

Before the day comes to an end I wish to have achieved:

1. --

2. --

3. --

CONTEMPLATE TODAY:

DO NOT GET SO BUSY MAKING A LIVING THAT YOU
FORGET TO MAKE A LIFE — DOLLY PARTON

CHALLENGE TOMORROW:

MAKE FUN PLANS WITH SOMEONE YOU LOVE

Three things I am thankful for today are:

1. --

2. --

3. --

Today I am proud of myself for:

My favourite moment of today was:

Tomorrow I am looking forward to:

DATE . ./. ./. .

Before the day comes to an end I wish to have achieved:

1. ---

2. ---

3. ---

CONTEMPLATE TODAY:

WHETHER YOU ARE KEEPING A JOURNAL OR WRITING AS A MEDITATION, IT IS THE SAME THING. WHAT IS IMPORTANT IS YOU ARE HAVING A RELATIONSHIP WITH YOUR MIND – NATALIE GOLDBERG

CHALLENGE TOMORROW:

MINDFULLY COMPLETE TODAY'S PAGE

Three things I am thankful for today are:

1. ---

2. ---

3. ---

Today I am proud of myself for:

My favourite moment of today was:

Tomorrow I am looking forward to:

DATE . ./. ./. .

Before the day comes to an end I wish to have achieved:

1. --

2. --

3. --

CONTEMPLATE TODAY:

ANY FOOL CAN CRITICISE, CONDEMN AND COMPLAIN
– AND MOST FOOLS DO – BENJAMIN FRANKLIN

CHALLENGE TOMORROW:

MAKE NO NEGATIVE REMARKS

Three things I am thankful for today are:

1. --

2. --

3. --

Today I am proud of myself for:

My favourite moment of today was:

Tomorrow I am looking forward to:

Nicely done!

Believe it or not you have just finished another 30 days! That is 60 days of your challenge completed, a wonderful achievement. Keep it up, you are doing amazing things.

REFLECTION

Before the day comes to an end I wish to have achieved:

1. ---

2. ---

3. ---

CONTEMPLATE TODAY:

WHAT CAN YOU GIVE REGULARLY THAT IS FREE?

CHALLENGE TOMORROW:

ANSWER THE ABOVE HERE:

Three things I am thankful for today are:

1. ---

2. ---

3. ---

Today I am proud of myself for:

My favourite moment of today was:

Tomorrow I am looking forward to:

DATE . ./. ./. .

Before the day comes to an end I wish to have achieved:

1. ....

2. ....

3. ....

CONTEMPLATE TODAY:

REGULAR WALKING HAS BEEN SHOWN TO
REDUCE THE RISKS OF CHRONIC ILLNESSES

CHALLENGE TOMORROW:
MAKE A PLAN HOW TO INCREASE YOUR
DAILY STEPS AND START IT

Three things I am thankful for today are:

1. ....

2. ....

3. ....

Today I am proud of myself for:

....

My favourite moment of today was:

....

Tomorrow I am looking forward to:

....

Before the day comes to an end I wish to have achieved:

1. --

2. --

3. --

CONTEMPLATE TODAY:

NURTURE YOUR MINDS WITH GREAT THOUGHTS. TO
BELIEVE IN THE HEROIC MAKES HEROES — BENJAMIN DISRAELI

CHALLENGE TOMORROW:
IMAGINE SOMETHING THAT MAKES YOU SMILE
AND KEEP REMINDING YOURSELF OF THAT

Three things I am thankful for today are:

1. --

2. --

3. --

Today I am proud of myself for:

My favourite moment of today was:

Tomorrow I am looking forward to:

DATE . ./. ./. .

Before the day comes to an end I wish to have achieved:

1. ....

2. ....

3. ....

CONTEMPLATE TODAY:

WHO ARE YOUR FAVOURITE PEOPLE
TO SPEND TIME WITH?

CHALLENGE TOMORROW:

WRITE DOWN THEIR NAMES HERE
AND THEN LET THEM KNOW

Three things I am thankful for today are:

1. ....

2. ....

3. ....

Today I am proud of myself for:

....

My favourite moment of today was:

....

Tomorrow I am looking forward to:

....

Before the day comes to an end I wish to have achieved:

1. --

2. --

3. --

CONTEMPLATE TODAY:

MINDFULNESS HAS BEEN PROVEN TO HELP WITH STRESS

CHALLENGE TOMORROW:

DO TWO FIVE-MINUTE MEDITATIONS

Three things I am thankful for today are:

1. --

2. --

3. --

Today I am proud of myself for:

My favourite moment of today was:

Tomorrow I am looking forward to:

DATE . ./. ./. .

Before the day comes to an end I wish to have achieved:

1. ---

2. ---

3. ---

CONTEMPLATE TODAY:

HAPPINESS IS A SKILL WE CAN LEARN

CHALLENGE TOMORROW:

TEACH YOURSELF SOMETHING NEW

Three things I am thankful for today are:

1. ---

2. ---

3. ---

Today I am proud of myself for:

My favourite moment of today was:

Tomorrow I am looking forward to:

Before the day comes to an end I wish to have achieved:

1. --

2. --

3. --

CONTEMPLATE TODAY:

EVERY GIFT FROM A FRIEND IS A WISH
FOR YOUR HAPPINESS — RICHARD BACH

CHALLENGE TOMORROW:

BUY YOURSELF A PRESENT

Three things I am thankful for today are:

1. --

2. --

3. --

Today I am proud of myself for:

My favourite moment of today was:

Tomorrow I am looking forward to:

DATE . ./. ./. .

Before the day comes to an end I wish to have achieved:

1. --

2. --

3. --

Three things I am thankful for today are:

1. --

2. --

3. --

Today I am proud of myself for:

My favourite moment of today was:

Tomorrow I am looking forward to:

Before the day comes to an end I wish to have achieved:

1. ....

2. ....

3. ....

CONTEMPLATE TODAY:

LAUGHTER RELEASES ENDORPHINS AND IS THEREFORE
A FREE PAINKILLER WITH NO SIDE EFFECTS

CHALLENGE TOMORROW:

VISIT WWW.TED.COM AND WATCH RUBY WAX'S
TALK ON MENTAL ILLNESS

Three things I am thankful for today are:

1. ....

2. ....

3. ....

Today I am proud of myself for:

....

My favourite moment of today was:

....

Tomorrow I am looking forward to:

....

DATE . ./. ./. .

Before the day comes to an end I wish to have achieved:

1. --

2. --

3. --

CONTEMPLATE TODAY:

REMEMBER THAT THE MOST VALUABLE ANTIQUES
ARE DEAR OLD FRIENDS – H. JACKSON BROWN, JR.

CHALLENGE TOMORROW:

CONTACT AN OLD FRIEND

Three things I am thankful for today are:

1. --

2. --

3. --

Today I am proud of myself for:

My favourite moment of today was:

Tomorrow I am looking forward to:

Before the day comes to an end I wish to have achieved:

1. ....

2. ....

3. ....

CONTEMPLATE TODAY:

MEDITATION IS PAINFUL IN THE BEGINNING BUT IT
BESTOWS IMMORTAL BLISS AND SUPREME JOY IN THE END
– SWAMI SIVANANDA

CHALLENGE TOMORROW:

DO A FIVE-MINUTE MINDFULNESS OF
THE BREATH EXERCISE

Three things I am thankful for today are:

1. ....

2. ....

3. ....

Today I am proud of myself for:

....

My favourite moment of today was:

....

Tomorrow I am looking forward to:

....

DATE . ./. ./. .

Before the day comes to an end I wish to have achieved:

1. --

2. --

3. --

CONTEMPLATE TODAY:

YOU ARE NEVER TOO OLD TO SET ANOTHER GOAL
OR TO DREAM A NEW DREAM – C. S. LEWIS

CHALLENGE TOMORROW:

DO SOMETHING THAT YOU HAVE BEEN
WANTING TO DO FOR AGES

Three things I am thankful for today are:

1. --

2. --

3. --

Today I am proud of myself for:

My favourite moment of today was:

Tomorrow I am looking forward to:

Before the day comes to an end I wish to have achieved:

1. ---

2. ---

3. ---

CONTEMPLATE TODAY:

HOW CAN YOU REGULARLY GIVE THE FREE THINGS
THAT YOU IDENTIFIED PREVIOUSLY?

CHALLENGE TOMORROW:

ANSWER THE ABOVE HERE:

Three things I am thankful for today are:

1. ---

2. ---

3. ---

Today I am proud of myself for:

My favourite moment of today was:

Tomorrow I am looking forward to:

DATE . ./. ./. .

Before the day comes to an end I wish to have achieved:

1. ---

2. ---

3. ---

CONTEMPLATE TODAY:

RESEARCH SHOWS THAT EXERCISE CAN BOOST MOOD

CHALLENGE TOMORROW:

WHEN YOU FEEL YOUR MOOD DIP, PUNCH THE AIR
60 TIMES (IN A CLEAR SPACE!)

Three things I am thankful for today are:

1. ---

2. ---

3. ---

Today I am proud of myself for:

My favourite moment of today was:

Tomorrow I am looking forward to:

Before the day comes to an end I wish to have achieved:

1. --

2. --

3. --

CONTEMPLATE TODAY:

WHAT WE NEED IS MORE PEOPLE WHO SPECIALISE
IN THE IMPOSSIBLE – THEODORE ROETHKE

CHALLENGE TOMORROW:
WRITE DOWN A GOAL YOU FEEL IS IMPOSSIBLE
BUT WOULD LOVE TO ACHIEVE

Three things I am thankful for today are:

1. --

2. --

3. --

Today I am proud of myself for:

My favourite moment of today was:

Tomorrow I am looking forward to:

DATE . ./. ./. .

Before the day comes to an end I wish to have achieved:

1. --

2. --

3. --

CONTEMPLATE TODAY:

OUR PERCEPTIONS ARE SUBJECTIVE

CHALLENGE TOMORROW:

VISIT WWW.TED.COM AND WATCH EMILY BALCETIS' TALK ON EXERCISE

Three things I am thankful for today are:

1. --

2. --

3. --

Today I am proud of myself for:

My favourite moment of today was:

Tomorrow I am looking forward to:

Before the day comes to an end I wish to have achieved:

1. --

2. --

3. --

CONTEMPLATE TODAY:

A THOUGHT IS NOT A FACT

CHALLENGE TOMORROW:

DO THREE FIVE-MINUTE MEDITATIONS

Three things I am thankful for today are:

1. --

2. --

3. --

Today I am proud of myself for:

My favourite moment of today was:

Tomorrow I am looking forward to:

DATE . ./. ./. .

Before the day comes to an end I wish to have achieved:

1. --

2. --

3. --

CONTEMPLATE TODAY:

40% OF OUR HAPPINESS CAN BE ATTRIBUTED TO OUR
DAILY ACTIVITIES AND CONSCIOUS CHOICES

CHALLENGE TOMORROW:

WAKE UP EARLIER THAN YOU NEED TO
AND EMBRACE THE DAY

Three things I am thankful for today are:

1. --

2. --

3. --

Today I am proud of myself for:

My favourite moment of today was:

Tomorrow I am looking forward to:

Before the day comes to an end I wish to have achieved:

1. --

2. --

3. --

CONTEMPLATE TODAY:

A HUG IS LIKE A BOOMERANG, YOU GET IT
BACK RIGHT AWAY – BIL KEANE

CHALLENGE TOMORROW:

GIVE AS MANY HUGS AS YOU CAN

Three things I am thankful for today are:

1. --

2. --

3. --

Today I am proud of myself for:

My favourite moment of today was:

Tomorrow I am looking forward to:

DATE . ./. ./. .

Before the day comes to an end I wish to have achieved:

1. ....

2. ....

3. ....

CONTEMPLATE TODAY:

RESEARCH SHOWS THAT EXERCISE CAN BOOST SELF-ESTEEM

CHALLENGE TOMORROW:

ARRANGE TO DO A PHYSICAL ACTIVITY WITH A FRIEND

Three things I am thankful for today are:

1. ....

2. ....

3. ....

Today I am proud of myself for:

....

My favourite moment of today was:

....

Tomorrow I am looking forward to:

....

Before the day comes to an end I wish to have achieved:

1. --

2. --

3. --

CONTEMPLATE TODAY:

WHAT WOULD YOU REALLY LIKE FROM YOUR LIFE?

CHALLENGE TOMORROW:

WRITE YOUR ANSWERS TO THE ABOVE HERE:

Three things I am thankful for today are:

1. --

2. --

3. --

Today I am proud of myself for:

My favourite moment of today was:

Tomorrow I am looking forward to:

DATE . . / . . / . .

Before the day comes to an end I wish to have achieved:

1. --

2. --

3. --

CONTEMPLATE TODAY:
THE LOVE OF FAMILY AND THE ADMIRATION OF FRIENDS
IS MUCH MORE IMPORTANT THAN WEALTH AND PRIVILEGE
– CHARLES KURALT

CHALLENGE TOMORROW:
WHEN YOU THINK ABOUT MONEY STOP AND SMILE AT
THOUGHTS OF YOUR FAMILY AND FRIENDS
INSTEAD

Three things I am thankful for today are:

1. --

2. --

3. --

Today I am proud of myself for:

My favourite moment of today was:

Tomorrow I am looking forward to:

Before the day comes to an end I wish to have achieved:

1. --

2. --

3. --

CONTEMPLATE TODAY:

MEDITATION MAKES THE ENTIRE NERVOUS SYSTEM GO INTO A FIELD OF COHERENCE – DEEPAK CHOPRA

CHALLENGE TOMORROW:

MEDITATE FOR 10 MINUTES

Three things I am thankful for today are:

1. --

2. --

3. --

Today I am proud of myself for:

My favourite moment of today was:

Tomorrow I am looking forward to:

DATE . ./. ./. .

Before the day comes to an end I wish to have achieved:

1. ....

2. ....

3. ....

CONTEMPLATE TODAY:

Take care of your body, you only get one

CHALLENGE TOMORROW:

Only consume home-cooked food from scratch

Three things I am thankful for today are:

1. ....

2. ....

3. ....

Today I am proud of myself for:

....

My favourite moment of today was:

....

Tomorrow I am looking forward to:

....

Before the day comes to an end I wish to have achieved:

1. --

2. --

3. --

CONTEMPLATE TODAY:

HOW OFTEN DO YOU GIVE UP CONTROL?

CHALLENGE TOMORROW:
VISIT WWW.TED.COM AND WATCH BABA SHIV'S TALK
ON GIVING UP THE DRIVER'S SEAT

Three things I am thankful for today are:

1. --

2. --

3. --

Today I am proud of myself for:

My favourite moment of today was:

Tomorrow I am looking forward to:

DATE . ./. ./. .

Before the day comes to an end I wish to have achieved:

1. --

2. --

3. --

CONTEMPLATE TODAY:

WALKING IS THE BEST POSSIBLE EXERCISE. HABITUATE
YOURSELF TO WALK VERY FAR – THOMAS JEFFERSON

CHALLENGE TOMORROW:

TAKE YOUR DOG FOR A LONG WALK,
EVEN IF YOU DO NOT HAVE A DOG

Three things I am thankful for today are:

1. --

2. --

3. --

Today I am proud of myself for:

My favourite moment of today was:

Tomorrow I am looking forward to:

Before the day comes to an end I wish to have achieved:

1. --

2. --

3. --

CONTEMPLATE TODAY:

WHAT COULD YOU DO TO BE KINDER TO YOURSELF?

CHALLENGE TOMORROW:

WRITE YOUR ANSWERS TO THE ABOVE HERE:

Three things I am thankful for today are:

1. --

2. --

3. --

Today I am proud of myself for:

My favourite moment of today was:

Tomorrow I am looking forward to:

DATE . . / . . / . .

Before the day comes to an end I wish to have achieved:

1. --

2. --

3. --

CONTEMPLATE TODAY:

WHAT KIND OF WORLD WOULD YOU LIKE TO LIVE IN?

CHALLENGE TOMORROW:

ANSWER THE ABOVE HERE:

Three things I am thankful for today are:

1. --

2. --

3. --

Today I am proud of myself for:

My favourite moment of today was:

Tomorrow I am looking forward to:

Before the day comes to an end I wish to have achieved:

1. --

2. --

3. --

CONTEMPLATE TODAY:

MINDFULNESS CAN HAVE A POSITIVE EFFECT ON PHYSICAL
PROBLEMS SUCH AS HEART DISEASE AND CHRONIC PAIN

CHALLENGE TOMORROW:

LISTEN TO VIVALDI'S FOUR SEASONS
(SPRING) MINDFULLY

Three things I am thankful for today are:

1. --

2. --

3. --

Today I am proud of myself for:

My favourite moment of today was:

Tomorrow I am looking forward to:

DATE . ./. ./. .

Before the day comes to an end I wish to have achieved:

1. --

2. --

3. --

CONTEMPLATE TODAY:

THE LESS ROUTINE THE MORE LIFE
– AMOS BRONSON ALCOTT

CHALLENGE TOMORROW:

CHOOSE A NEW WAY TO GET TO SOMEWHERE
YOU REGULARLY GO

Three things I am thankful for today are:

1. --

2. --

3. --

Today I am proud of myself for:

My favourite moment of today was:

Tomorrow I am looking forward to:

HALF WAY!

Welcome half way heroes, hats off to your latest victory. You have now accomplished 90 days on your quest to a happier and healthier lifestyle. By now the process will be becoming more of a habit which is great news for everyone. All you have left to do is exactly what you have just achieved so make it count.

REFLECTION

Before the day comes to an end I wish to have achieved:

1. ---

2. ---

3. ---

CONTEMPLATE TODAY:

KIND WORDS DO NOT COST MUCH. YET THEY
ACCOMPLISH MUCH – BLAISE PASCAL

CHALLENGE TOMORROW:

GIVE YOURSELF COMPLIMENTS

Three things I am thankful for today are:

1. ---

2. ---

3. ---

Today I am proud of myself for:

My favourite moment of today was:

Tomorrow I am looking forward to:

DATE . ./. ./. .

Before the day comes to an end I wish to have achieved:

1. --

2. --

3. --

CONTEMPLATE TODAY:

HEALTH IS THE VITAL PRINCIPLE OF BLISS,
AND EXERCISE, OF HEALTH — JAMES THOMSON

CHALLENGE TOMORROW:

DO A 20-MINUTE LIGHT JOG

Three things I am thankful for today are:

1. --

2. --

3. --

Today I am proud of myself for:

My favourite moment of today was:

Tomorrow I am looking forward to:

Before the day comes to an end I wish to have achieved:

1. --

2. --

3. --

CONTEMPLATE TODAY:

WHAT DOES GREAT 'ME' TIME MEAN TO YOU?

CHALLENGE TOMORROW:

WRITE YOUR ANSWERS TO THE ABOVE HERE:

Three things I am thankful for today are:

1. --

2. --

3. --

Today I am proud of myself for:

My favourite moment of today was:

Tomorrow I am looking forward to:

DATE . ./. ./. .

Before the day comes to an end I wish to have achieved:

1. ....

2. ....

3. ....

CONTEMPLATE TODAY:

THERE ARE NO STRANGERS HERE; ONLY FRIENDS YOU HAVE NOT MET YET – WILLIAM BUTLER YEATS

CHALLENGE TOMORROW:

MAKE A NEW FRIEND

Three things I am thankful for today are:

1. ....

2. ....

3. ....

Today I am proud of myself for:

....

My favourite moment of today was:

....

Tomorrow I am looking forward to:

....

Before the day comes to an end I wish to have achieved:

1. --

2. --

3. --

CONTEMPLATE TODAY:

THIS IS LOVE: THE FLOWERING OF LOVE IS MEDITATION
— JIDDU KRISHNAMURTI

CHALLENGE TOMORROW:

MEDITATE FOR 10 MINUTES

Three things I am thankful for today are:

1. --

2. --

3. --

Today I am proud of myself for:

My favourite moment of today was:

Tomorrow I am looking forward to:

DATE . ./. ./. .

Before the day comes to an end I wish to have achieved:

1. ---

2. ---

3. ---

CONTEMPLATE TODAY:

LIFE IS NOT A PROBLEM TO BE SOLVED, BUT A REALITY
TO BE EXPERIENCED — SOREN KIERKGAARD

CHALLENGE TOMORROW:

VISIT A NEW PLACE

Three things I am thankful for today are:

1. ---

2. ---

3. ---

Today I am proud of myself for:

My favourite moment of today was:

Tomorrow I am looking forward to:

Before the day comes to an end I wish to have achieved:

1. ---

2. ---

3. ---

CONTEMPLATE TODAY:

THINK OF SOMETHING THAT DEPENDS ON YOU FOR SURVIVAL

CHALLENGE TOMORROW:

PURPOSEFULLY GIVE THE ABOVE ALL THE CARE AND ATTENTION IT NEEDS

Three things I am thankful for today are:

1. ---

2. ---

3. ---

Today I am proud of myself for:

My favourite moment of today was:

Tomorrow I am looking forward to:

DATE . ./. ./. .

Before the day comes to an end I wish to have achieved:

1. --

2. --

3. --

CONTEMPLATE TODAY:

YOU WOULD NOT BE ABLE TO WALK ON JUPITER, SATURN,
URANUS OR NEPTUNE BECAUSE THEY HAVE NO SOLID SURFACE

CHALLENGE TOMORROW:

GO FOR A 30-MINUTE WALK AMONG
AS MUCH NATURE AS POSSIBLE

Three things I am thankful for today are:

1. --

2. --

3. --

Today I am proud of myself for:

My favourite moment of today was:

Tomorrow I am looking forward to:

Before the day comes to an end I wish to have achieved:

1. --

2. --

3. --

CONTEMPLATE TODAY:

ONLY PASSIONS, GREAT PASSIONS CAN ELEVATE THE
SOUL TO GREAT THINGS — DENIS DIDEROT

CHALLENGE TOMORROW:

WRITE DOWN YOUR MAIN PASSION HERE:

Three things I am thankful for today are:

1. --

2. --

3. --

Today I am proud of myself for:

My favourite moment of today was:

Tomorrow I am looking forward to:

DATE . ./. ./. .

Before the day comes to an end I wish to have achieved:

1. ---

2. ---

3. ---

CONTEMPLATE TODAY:

HOW DO YOU CONNECT WITH YOUR NEIGHBOURS?

CHALLENGE TOMORROW:

VISIT WWW.TED.COM AND WATCH CANDY CHANG'S TALK ON BEFORE I DIE

Three things I am thankful for today are:

1. ---

2. ---

3. ---

Today I am proud of myself for:

My favourite moment of today was:

Tomorrow I am looking forward to:

Before the day comes to an end I wish to have achieved:

1. --

2. --

3. --

CONTEMPLATE TODAY:

MINDFULNESS HELPS YOU GO HOME TO THE PRESENT. AND EVERY
TIME YOU GO THERE AND RECOGNISE A CONDITION OF HAPPINESS THAT
YOU HAVE, HAPPINESS COMES – NHAT HANH

CHALLENGE TOMORROW:

LISTEN TO BEETHOVEN'S MOONLIGHT SONATA
MINDFULLY

Three things I am thankful for today are:

1. --

2. --

3. --

Today I am proud of myself for:

My favourite moment of today was:

Tomorrow I am looking forward to:

DATE . ./. ./. .

Before the day comes to an end I wish to have achieved:

1. ---

2. ---

3. ---

CONTEMPLATE TODAY:

THE FUTURE STARTS TODAY

CHALLENGE TOMORROW:
THINK OF SOMETHING YOU WANT
AND MAKE IT HAPPEN

Three things I am thankful for today are:

1. ---

2. ---

3. ---

Today I am proud of myself for:

My favourite moment of today was:

Tomorrow I am looking forward to:

Before the day comes to an end I wish to have achieved:

1. --

2. --

3. --

CONTEMPLATE TODAY:

EVERY MAN MUST DECIDE WHETHER HE WILL WALK IN THE LIGHT OF CREATIVE ALTRUISM OR IN THE DARKNESS OF DESTRUCTIVE SELFISHNESS – MARTIN LUTHER KING, JR

CHALLENGE TOMORROW:

BUY A STRANGER A SMALL GIFT

Three things I am thankful for today are:

1. --

2. --

3. --

Today I am proud of myself for:

My favourite moment of today was:

Tomorrow I am looking forward to:

DATE . ./. ./. .

Before the day comes to an end I wish to have achieved:

1. --

2. --

3. --

CONTEMPLATE TODAY:
EXERCISE TO STIMULATE, NOT ANNIHILATE. THE WORLD WAS
NOT FORMED IN A DAY AND NEITHER WERE WE. SET SMALL GOALS
AND BUILD UPON THEM – LEE HANEY
CHALLENGE TOMORROW:
DO AS MANY SQUATS THROUGHOUT THE DAY AS YOU
CAN, WRITE DOWN YOUR TOTAL HERE:

Three things I am thankful for today are:

1. --

2. --

3. --

Today I am proud of myself for:

My favourite moment of today was:

Tomorrow I am looking forward to:

Before the day comes to an end I wish to have achieved:

1. --

2. --

3. --

CONTEMPLATE TODAY:

DO NOT JUDGE EACH DAY BY THE HARVEST YOU REAP BUT
BY THE SEEDS THAT YOU PLANT – ROBERT LOUIS STEVENSON

CHALLENGE TOMORROW:

BUY A SEED OR A PLANT, LOOK AFTER IT,
WATCH IT GROW

Three things I am thankful for today are:

1. --

2. --

3. --

Today I am proud of myself for:

My favourite moment of today was:

Tomorrow I am looking forward to:

DATE . ./. ./. .

Before the day comes to an end I wish to have achieved:

1. ---

2. ---

3. ---

CONTEMPLATE TODAY:
IF YOU WANT TO DO REALLY IMPORTANT THINGS IN LIFE, YOU
CANNOT DO ANYTHING BY YOURSELF. AND YOUR BEST TEAMS ARE YOUR
FRIENDS AND YOUR SIBLINGS – DEEPAK CHOPRA

CHALLENGE TOMORROW:
MAKE A PLAN TO ACHIEVE SOMETHING
WITH THOSE CLOSEST TO YOU

Three things I am thankful for today are:

1. ---

2. ---

3. ---

Today I am proud of myself for:

My favourite moment of today was:

Tomorrow I am looking forward to:

Before the day comes to an end I wish to have achieved:

1. ....

2. ....

3. ....

CONTEMPLATE TODAY:

MINDFULNESS CAN BE PRACTISED BY ANYONE WHO WANTS TO

CHALLENGE TOMORROW:

MEDITATE FOR 15 MINUTES

Three things I am thankful for today are:

1. ....

2. ....

3. ....

Today I am proud of myself for:

....

My favourite moment of today was:

....

Tomorrow I am looking forward to:

....

DATE . ./. ./. .

Before the day comes to an end I wish to have achieved:

1. --

2. --

3. --

CONTEMPLATE TODAY:

NO ACT OF KINDNESS, NO MATTER HOW SMALL,
IS EVER WASTED – AESOP

CHALLENGE TOMORROW:

BE VEGETARIAN FOR THE DAY

Three things I am thankful for today are:

1. --

2. --

3. --

Today I am proud of myself for:

My favourite moment of today was:

Tomorrow I am looking forward to:

Before the day comes to an end I wish to have achieved:

1. ....

2. ....

3. ....

CONTEMPLATE TODAY:

IF YOU WANT TO FEEL GOOD, DO GOOD

CHALLENGE TOMORROW:

DO A GREAT DEED

Three things I am thankful for today are:

1. ....

2. ....

3. ....

Today I am proud of myself for:

....

My favourite moment of today was:

....

Tomorrow I am looking forward to:

....

DATE . ./. ./. .

Before the day comes to an end I wish to have achieved:

1. --

2. --

3. --

CONTEMPLATE TODAY:
IT IS MEDICALLY PROVEN THAT PEOPLE WHO DO REGULAR
PHYSICAL ACTIVITY HAVE UP TO A 83% LOWER
RISK OF OSTEOARTHRITIS

CHALLENGE TOMORROW:
DO 20 MINUTES OF EXERCISE THAT
YOU FIND RELATIVELY HARD

Three things I am thankful for today are:

1. --

2. --

3. --

Today I am proud of myself for:

My favourite moment of today was:

Tomorrow I am looking forward to:

Before the day comes to an end I wish to have achieved:

1. --

2. --

3. --

CONTEMPLATE TODAY:

IN THE NEXT YEAR WHAT WOULD YOU
LIKE TO ACHIEVE?

CHALLENGE TOMORROW:
WRITE YOUR ANSWERS TO THE ABOVE HERE:

Three things I am thankful for today are:

1. --

2. --

3. --

Today I am proud of myself for:

My favourite moment of today was:

Tomorrow I am looking forward to:

DATE . ./. ./. .

Before the day comes to an end I wish to have achieved:

1. --

2. --

3. --

Three things I am thankful for today are:

1. --

2. --

3. --

Today I am proud of myself for:

My favourite moment of today was:

Tomorrow I am looking forward to:

Before the day comes to an end I wish to have achieved:

1. --

2. --

3. --

CONTEMPLATE TODAY:

INCORPORATING MINDFULNESS INTO YOUR LIFE CAN BE EASY

CHALLENGE TOMORROW:

WHEN YOU EAT, DO IT MINDFULLY

Three things I am thankful for today are:

1. --

2. --

3. --

Today I am proud of myself for:

My favourite moment of today was:

Tomorrow I am looking forward to:

Before the day comes to an end I wish to have achieved:

1. --

2. --

3. --

CONTEMPLATE TODAY:

POSITIVE EMOTIONS MAKE US MORE RESILIENT

CHALLENGE TOMORROW:

COOK A NEW HEALTHY RECIPE THAT WILL MAKE YOU FEEL GOOD

Three things I am thankful for today are:

1. --

2. --

3. --

Today I am proud of myself for:

My favourite moment of today was:

Tomorrow I am looking forward to:

Before the day comes to an end I wish to have achieved:

1. --

2. --

3. --

CONTEMPLATE TODAY:

WE MAKE A LIVING BY WHAT WE GET, BUT WE MAKE A
LIFE BY WHAT WE GIVE — WINSTON CHURCHILL

CHALLENGE TOMORROW:

FIND A WAY TO GIVE YOUR TIME TO
SOMEONE IN NEED AND DO IT

Three things I am thankful for today are:

1. --

2. --

3. --

Today I am proud of myself for:

My favourite moment of today was:

Tomorrow I am looking forward to:

DATE . ./. ./. .

Before the day comes to an end I wish to have achieved:

1. ....

2. ....

3. ....

CONTEMPLATE TODAY:
IF IT WERE NOT FOR THE FACT THAT THE TV SET AND
REFRIGERATOR ARE SO FAR APART, SOME OF US WOULD NOT GET
ANY EXERCISE AT ALL – JOEY ADAMS
CHALLENGE TOMORROW:
DO AS MANY STAR JUMPS THROUGHOUT THE DAY
AS YOU CAN, WRITE DOWN YOUR TOTAL HERE:

Three things I am thankful for today are:

1. ....

2. ....

3. ....

Today I am proud of myself for:

....

My favourite moment of today was:

....

Tomorrow I am looking forward to:

....

Before the day comes to an end I wish to have achieved:

1. --

2. --

3. --

CONTEMPLATE TODAY:

OUR LIFE ALWAYS EXPRESSES THE RESULT OF OUR
DOMINANT THOUGHTS – SOREN KIERKEGAARD

CHALLENGE TOMORROW:

THINK WHAT YOU WANT YOUR LIFE TO
EXPRESS AND KEEP THINKING IT

Three things I am thankful for today are:

1. --

2. --

3. --

Today I am proud of myself for:

My favourite moment of today was:

Tomorrow I am looking forward to:

DATE . ./. ./. .

Before the day comes to an end I wish to have achieved:

1. ....

2. ....

3. ....

CONTEMPLATE TODAY:

Friendships change with time

CHALLENGE TOMORROW:

Accept that everything is temporary and that this is okay

Three things I am thankful for today are:

1. ....

2. ....

3. ....

Today I am proud of myself for:

....

My favourite moment of today was:

....

Tomorrow I am looking forward to:

....

Before the day comes to an end I wish to have achieved:

1. --

2. --

3. --

CONTEMPLATE TODAY:

YOGA IS A WAY TO FREEDOM. BY ITS CONSTANT PRACTICE,
WE CAN FREE OURSELVES FROM FEAR, ANGUISH
AND LONELINESS – INDRA DEVI

CHALLENGE TOMORROW:

FIND A YOGA CLASS YOU WANT TO ATTEND,
BOOK IT

Three things I am thankful for today are:

1. --

2. --

3. --

Today I am proud of myself for:

My favourite moment of today was:

Tomorrow I am looking forward to:

DATE . ./. ./. .

Before the day comes to an end I wish to have achieved:

1. ....

2. ....

3. ....

CONTEMPLATE TODAY:

BELIEVE YOU CAN AND YOU ARE HALFWAY THERE
– THEODORE ROOSEVELT

CHALLENGE TOMORROW:
WHEN YOU FIND YOURSELF SAYING I CANNOT,
CHANGE IT TO I CAN

Three things I am thankful for today are:

1. ....

2. ....

3. ....

Today I am proud of myself for:

....

My favourite moment of today was:

....

Tomorrow I am looking forward to:

....

WELL DONE!

Just like that, you are another 30 days down. Never underestimate the work you have done to get to this magnificent point. Look over the first few sections and see how far you have come.

REFLECTION

Before the day comes to an end I wish to have achieved:

1. --

2. --

3. --

CONTEMPLATE TODAY:

HOW OFTEN DO YOU DECIDE NOT TO
SQUISH AN INSECT?

CHALLENGE TOMORROW:

GIVE LIFE, SAVE A BUG

Three things I am thankful for today are:

1. --

2. --

3. --

Today I am proud of myself for:

My favourite moment of today was:

Tomorrow I am looking forward to:

DATE . ./. ./. .

Before the day comes to an end I wish to have achieved:

1. --

2. --

3. --

CONTEMPLATE TODAY:

HAPPINESS FUELS SUCCESS NOT THE
OTHER WAY ROUND

CHALLENGE TOMORROW:

GO FOR A 40-MINUTE WALK
IN NATURE

Three things I am thankful for today are:

1. --

2. --

3. --

Today I am proud of myself for:

My favourite moment of today was:

Tomorrow I am looking forward to:

Before the day comes to an end I wish to have achieved:

1. --

2. --

3. --

CONTEMPLATE TODAY:

IN THE NEXT FIVE YEARS WHAT WOULD YOU LIKE TO ACHIEVE?

CHALLENGE TOMORROW:

WRITE YOUR ANSWERS TO THE ABOVE HERE:

Three things I am thankful for today are:

1. --

2. --

3. --

Today I am proud of myself for:

My favourite moment of today was:

Tomorrow I am looking forward to:

DATE . ./. ./. .

Before the day comes to an end I wish to have achieved:

1. --

2. --

3. --

CONTEMPLATE TODAY:
FRIENDSHIP IS THE SOURCE OF THE GREATEST PLEASURES,
AND WITHOUT FRIENDS EVEN THE MOST AGREEABLE
PURSUITS BECOME TEDIOUS – THOMAS AQUINAS
CHALLENGE TOMORROW:
THINK OF SOMETHING YOU ARE PLANNING TO DO
BY YOURSELF, INVITE A FRIEND ALONG

Three things I am thankful for today are:

1. --

2. --

3. --

Today I am proud of myself for:

My favourite moment of today was:

Tomorrow I am looking forward to:

Before the day comes to an end I wish to have achieved:

1. --

2. --

3. --

CONTEMPLATE TODAY:

MINDFULNESS HAS BEEN PROVEN TO
HELP WITH DEPRESSION

CHALLENGE TOMORROW:

CHOOSE THREE THINGS TO DO MINDFULLY

Three things I am thankful for today are:

1. --

2. --

3. --

Today I am proud of myself for:

My favourite moment of today was:

Tomorrow I am looking forward to:

DATE . ./. ./. .

Before the day comes to an end I wish to have achieved:

1. ....

2. ....

3. ....

CONTEMPLATE TODAY:

HABITS CAN BE ALTERED

CHALLENGE TOMORROW:

TAKE A DIFFERENT APPROACH TO FILLING IN TODAY'S PAGE

Three things I am thankful for today are:

1. ....

2. ....

3. ....

Today I am proud of myself for:
....

My favourite moment of today was:
....

Tomorrow I am looking forward to:
....

Before the day comes to an end I wish to have achieved:

1. --

2. --

3. --

CONTEMPLATE TODAY:

HAPPINESS RESIDES NOT IN POSSESSIONS, AND NOT IN GOLD, HAPPINESS DWELLS IN THE SOUL – Democritus

CHALLENGE TOMORROW:

DONATE SOMETHING YOU OWN

Three things I am thankful for today are:

1. --

2. --

3. --

Today I am proud of myself for:

My favourite moment of today was:

Tomorrow I am looking forward to:

DATE . ./. ./. .

Before the day comes to an end I wish to have achieved:

1. --

2. --

3. --

CONTEMPLATE TODAY:

BELIEVE THAT LIFE IS WORTH LIVING AND YOUR BELIEF
WILL HELP CREATE THE FACT —WILLIAM JAMES

CHALLENGE TOMORROW:

GO FOR A 30-MINUTE WALK IN NATURE
EMBRACING EVERY STEP

Three things I am thankful for today are:

1. --

2. --

3. --

Today I am proud of myself for:

My favourite moment of today was:

Tomorrow I am looking forward to:

Before the day comes to an end I wish to have achieved:

1. --

2. --

3. --

CONTEMPLATE TODAY:
MY PAIN MAY BE THE REASON FOR SOMEBODY'S LAUGH BUT
MY LAUGH MUST NEVER BE THE REASON FOR SOMEBODY'S PAIN –
CHARLIE CHAPLIN

CHALLENGE TOMORROW:
MAKE SOMEONE LAUGH

Three things I am thankful for today are:

1. --

2. --

3. --

Today I am proud of myself for:

My favourite moment of today was:

Tomorrow I am looking forward to:

DATE . ./. ./. .

Before the day comes to an end I wish to have achieved:

1. ---

2. ---

3. ---

CONTEMPLATE TODAY:

NOT ALL SOCIETIES ARE THE SAME

CHALLENGE TOMORROW:

VISIT WWW.TED.COM AND WATCH DAN BUETTNER'S TALK ON HOW TO LIVE TO BE 100+

Three things I am thankful for today are:

1. ---

2. ---

3. ---

Today I am proud of myself for:

My favourite moment of today was:

Tomorrow I am looking forward to:

Before the day comes to an end I wish to have achieved:

1. --

2. --

3. --

CONTEMPLATE TODAY:

SLEEP IS THE BEST MEDITATION – DALAI LAMA

CHALLENGE TOMORROW:

MINDFULLY GO TO BED EARLY

Three things I am thankful for today are:

1. --

2. --

3. --

Today I am proud of myself for:

My favourite moment of today was:

Tomorrow I am looking forward to:

DATE . ./. ./. .

Before the day comes to an end I wish to have achieved:

1. --

2. --

3. --

CONTEMPLATE TODAY:

ANYONE WHO KEEPS THE ABILITY TO SEE BEAUTY
NEVER GROWS OLD – FRANZ KAFKA

CHALLENGE TOMORROW:

DO NOT WATCH TELEVISION

Three things I am thankful for today are:

1. --

2. --

3. --

Today I am proud of myself for:

My favourite moment of today was:

Tomorrow I am looking forward to:

Before the day comes to an end I wish to have achieved:

1. --

2. --

3. --

CONTEMPLATE TODAY:

WHAT ARE YOUR MAIN TALENTS?

CHALLENGE TOMORROW:
CREATE A PLAN TO USE YOUR TALENTS TO GIVE BACK TO THE WORLD

Three things I am thankful for today are:

1. --

2. --

3. --

Today I am proud of myself for:

My favourite moment of today was:

Tomorrow I am looking forward to:

DATE . ./. ./. .

Before the day comes to an end I wish to have achieved:

1. ....

2. ....

3. ....

CONTEMPLATE TODAY:
TRUE ENJOYMENT COMES FROM ACTIVITY OF THE MIND
AND EXERCISE OF THE BODY; THE TWO ARE EVER UNITED
– WILHELM VON HUMBOLDT
CHALLENGE TOMORROW:
JOG ON THE SPOT WHENEVER YOU
ARE ABLE TO

Three things I am thankful for today are:

1. ....

2. ....

3. ....

Today I am proud of myself for:

....

My favourite moment of today was:

....

Tomorrow I am looking forward to:

....

Before the day comes to an end I wish to have achieved:

1. --

2. --

3. --

CONTEMPLATE TODAY:

IN THE NEXT 10 YEARS
WHAT WOULD YOU LIKE TO ACHIEVE?

CHALLENGE TOMORROW:
WRITE YOUR ANSWERS TO THE ABOVE HERE:

Three things I am thankful for today are:

1. --

2. --

3. --

Today I am proud of myself for:

My favourite moment of today was:

Tomorrow I am looking forward to:

DATE . ./. ./. .

Before the day comes to an end I wish to have achieved:

1. --

2. --

3. --

CONTEMPLATE TODAY:

ISOLATION IS PHYSICALLY BAD FOR US

CHALLENGE TOMORROW:

PURPOSEFULLY SURROUND YOURSELF WITH PEOPLE

Three things I am thankful for today are:

1. --

2. --

3. --

Today I am proud of myself for:

My favourite moment of today was:

Tomorrow I am looking forward to:

Before the day comes to an end I wish to have achieved:

1. --

2. --

3. --

CONTEMPLATE TODAY:

MINDFULNESS IS FREE FOR THOSE WHO KNOW HOW TO ACCESS IT

CHALLENGE TOMORROW:
ASK THREE PEOPLE WHAT THEY KNOW ABOUT MINDFULNESS, TEACH THEM SOMETHING NEW

Three things I am thankful for today are:

1. --

2. --

3. --

Today I am proud of myself for:

My favourite moment of today was:

Tomorrow I am looking forward to:

DATE . ./. ./. .

Before the day comes to an end I wish to have achieved:

1. ....

2. ....

3. ....

CONTEMPLATE TODAY:

A WORRY IS JUST THAT

CHALLENGE TOMORROW:

WRITE YOUR WORRIES DOWN ON A PIECE OF
PAPER AND THEN DISPOSE OF IT

Three things I am thankful for today are:

1. ....

2. ....

3. ....

Today I am proud of myself for:
....

My favourite moment of today was:
....

Tomorrow I am looking forward to:
....

Before the day comes to an end I wish to have achieved:

1. --

2. --

3. --

CONTEMPLATE TODAY:

No one is useless in this world who lightens the burden of it to anyone else – Charles Dickens

CHALLENGE TOMORROW:

Help someone who is less able than yourself

Three things I am thankful for today are:

1. --

2. --

3. --

Today I am proud of myself for:

My favourite moment of today was:

Tomorrow I am looking forward to:

DATE . ./. ./. .

Before the day comes to an end I wish to have achieved:

1. --

2. --

3. --

CONTEMPLATE TODAY:

Exercise is free and requires no prescription

CHALLENGE TOMORROW:

Go for a 30-minute swim

Three things I am thankful for today are:

1. --

2. --

3. --

Today I am proud of myself for:

My favourite moment of today was:

Tomorrow I am looking forward to:

Before the day comes to an end I wish to have achieved:

1. --

2. --

3. --

CONTEMPLATE TODAY:

IF YOU HAVE 24 HOURS TO LIVE,
HOW WOULD YOU SPEND IT?

CHALLENGE TOMORROW:

WRITE YOUR ANSWERS TO THE ABOVE HERE:

Three things I am thankful for today are:

1. --

2. --

3. --

Today I am proud of myself for:

My favourite moment of today was:

Tomorrow I am looking forward to:

DATE . ./. ./. .

Before the day comes to an end I wish to have achieved:

1. ---

2. ---

3. ---

CONTEMPLATE TODAY:

THE BEST TIME TO MAKE FRIENDS IS BEFORE YOU NEED THEM – ETHEL BARRYMORE

CHALLENGE TOMORROW:

FIND A GROUP/ORGANISATION THAT YOU WOULD LIKE TO BE A PART OF, JOIN IT

Three things I am thankful for today are:

1. ---

2. ---

3. ---

Today I am proud of myself for:

My favourite moment of today was:

Tomorrow I am looking forward to:

Before the day comes to an end I wish to have achieved:

1. --

2. --

3. --

CONTEMPLATE TODAY:

THE FIRST RECIPE FOR HAPPINESS IS: AVOID TOO
LENGTHY MEDITATION ON THE PAST – ANDRE MAUROIS

CHALLENGE TOMORROW:

DO FOUR FIVE-MINUTE MEDITATIONS

Three things I am thankful for today are:

1. --

2. --

3. --

Today I am proud of myself for:

My favourite moment of today was:

Tomorrow I am looking forward to:

DATE . ./. ./. .

Before the day comes to an end I wish to have achieved:

1. ....

2. ....

3. ....

CONTEMPLATE TODAY:

Life is

CHALLENGE TOMORROW:

Finish the above

Three things I am thankful for today are:

1. ....

2. ....

3. ....

Today I am proud of myself for:

....

My favourite moment of today was:

....

Tomorrow I am looking forward to:

....

Before the day comes to an end I wish to have achieved:

1. --

2. --

3. --

CONTEMPLATE TODAY:

YOU CAN ALWAYS GIVE

CHALLENGE TOMORROW:
CHOOSE A RANDOM TIME TODAY, NO MATTER WHERE
YOU END UP BEING, FIND A WAY TO GIVE

Three things I am thankful for today are:

1. --

2. --

3. --

Today I am proud of myself for:

My favourite moment of today was:

Tomorrow I am looking forward to:

DATE . ./. ./. .

Before the day comes to an end I wish to have achieved:

1. ....

2. ....

3. ....

CONTEMPLATE TODAY:

RESEARCH SHOWS THAT EXERCISE
CAN BOOST SLEEP QUALITY

CHALLENGE TOMORROW:

BEFORE DINNER DO 30 MINUTES
OF EXERCISE

Three things I am thankful for today are:

1. ....

2. ....

3. ....

Today I am proud of myself for:

....

My favourite moment of today was:

....

Tomorrow I am looking forward to:

....

Before the day comes to an end I wish to have achieved:

1. --

2. --

3. --

CONTEMPLATE TODAY:
IF YOU NURTURE YOUR MIND, BODY AND SPIRIT, YOUR
TIME WILL EXPAND. YOU WILL GAIN A NEW PERSPECTIVE THAT WILL
ALLOW YOU TO ACCOMPLISH MUCH MORE – BRIAN KOSLOW
CHALLENGE TOMORROW:
BE KIND TO YOURSELF USING THE WAYS
YOU IDENTIFIED PREVIOUSLY

Three things I am thankful for today are:

1. --

2. --

3. --

Today I am proud of myself for:

My favourite moment of today was:

Tomorrow I am looking forward to:

DATE . ./. ./. .

Before the day comes to an end I wish to have achieved:

1. ....

2. ....

3. ....

CONTEMPLATE TODAY:

DO YOU REGARD PHYSICAL HEALTH AS IMPORTANT AS MENTAL HEALTH?

CHALLENGE TOMORROW:
VISIT WWW.TED.COM AND WATCH GUY WINCH'S TALK ON EMOTIONAL FIRST-AID

Three things I am thankful for today are:

1. ....

2. ....

3. ....

Today I am proud of myself for:

....

My favourite moment of today was:

....

Tomorrow I am looking forward to:

....

Before the day comes to an end I wish to have achieved:

1. --

2. --

3. --

CONTEMPLATE TODAY:

MINDFULNESS HAS BEEN PROVEN TO HELP WITH ANXIETY

CHALLENGE TOMORROW:

CHOOSE YOUR FAVOURITE MEDITATION TO DO FOR 20 MINUTES

Three things I am thankful for today are:

1. --

2. --

3. --

Today I am proud of myself for:

My favourite moment of today was:

Tomorrow I am looking forward to:

DATE . ./. ./. .

Before the day comes to an end I wish to have achieved:

1. --

2. --

3. --

Three things I am thankful for today are:

1. --

2. --

3. --

Today I am proud of myself for:

My favourite moment of today was:

Tomorrow I am looking forward to:

NEARLY THERE!

After all your hard work the final 30 days are here, embrace each one as your challenge is very nearly complete.

REFLECTION

Before the day comes to an end I wish to have achieved:

1. --

2. --

3. --

CONTEMPLATE TODAY:

EVERY ACTION IN OUR LIVES TOUCHES ON SOME CHORD
THAT WILL VIBRATE IN ETERNITY – EDWIN HUBBEL CHAPIN

CHALLENGE TOMORROW:

SIGN UP TO VOLUNTEER

Three things I am thankful for today are:

1. --

2. --

3. --

Today I am proud of myself for:

My favourite moment of today was:

Tomorrow I am looking forward to:

DATE . ./. ./. .

Before the day comes to an end I wish to have achieved:

1. ....

2. ....

3. ....

CONTEMPLATE TODAY:

THE REASON I EXERCISE IS FOR THE QUALITY OF LIFE
I ENJOY – KENNETH H. COOPER

CHALLENGE TOMORROW:

DO 30 MINUTES OF YOUR FAVOURITE EXERCISE

Three things I am thankful for today are:

1. ....

2. ....

3. ....

Today I am proud of myself for:

....

My favourite moment of today was:

....

Tomorrow I am looking forward to:

....

Before the day comes to an end I wish to have achieved:

1. --

2. --

3. --

CONTEMPLATE TODAY:

IF EVERYONE YOU SAW TODAY HAD 24 HOURS TO LIVE,
HOW WOULD YOU TREAT THEM?

CHALLENGE TOMORROW:

WRITE YOUR ANSWERS TO THE ABOVE HERE:

Three things I am thankful for today are:

1. --

2. --

3. --

Today I am proud of myself for:

My favourite moment of today was:

Tomorrow I am looking forward to:

DATE . ./. ./. .

Before the day comes to an end I wish to have achieved:

1. ---

2. ---

3. ---

CONTEMPLATE TODAY:

FRIENDSHIP WITH ONE'S SELF IS ALL IMPORTANT,
BECAUSE WITHOUT IT ONE CANNOT BE FRIENDS WITH ANYONE
ELSE IN THE WORLD – ELEANOR ROOSEVELT

CHALLENGE TOMORROW:

TREAT YOURSELF HOW YOU WOULD LIKE
YOUR BEST FRIEND TO TREAT YOU

Three things I am thankful for today are:

1. ---

2. ---

3. ---

Today I am proud of myself for:

My favourite moment of today was:

Tomorrow I am looking forward to:

Before the day comes to an end I wish to have achieved:

1. --

2. --

3. --

CONTEMPLATE TODAY:

HALF AN HOUR'S MEDITATION EACH DAY IS ESSENTIAL,
EXCEPT WHEN YOU ARE BUSY. THEN A FULL HOUR IS NEEDED –
SAINT FRANCIS DE SALES

CHALLENGE TOMORROW:

DO THREE 10-MINUTE MEDITATIONS

Three things I am thankful for today are:

1. --

2. --

3. --

Today I am proud of myself for:

My favourite moment of today was:

Tomorrow I am looking forward to:

DATE . ./. ./. .

Before the day comes to an end I wish to have achieved:

1. --

2. --

3. --

CONTEMPLATE TODAY:

ACCEPT THE CHALLENGES SO THAT YOU CAN FEEL THE
EXHILARATION OF VICTORY – GEORGE S. PATTON

CHALLENGE TOMORROW:

TAKE A COLD SHOWER

Three things I am thankful for today are:

1. --

2. --

3. --

Today I am proud of myself for:

My favourite moment of today was:

Tomorrow I am looking forward to:

Before the day comes to an end I wish to have achieved:

1. --

2. --

3. --

CONTEMPLATE TODAY:

WHO DO YOU FEEL IN YOUR SOCIETY IS IN NEED?

CHALLENGE TOMORROW:

CREATE A WAY TO GIVE TO THOSE IDENTIFIED ABOVE

Three things I am thankful for today are:

1. --

2. --

3. --

Today I am proud of myself for:

My favourite moment of today was:

Tomorrow I am looking forward to:

DATE . ./. ./. .

Before the day comes to an end I wish to have achieved:

1. --

2. --

3. --

CONTEMPLATE TODAY:

IT IS MEDICALLY PROVEN THAT PEOPLE WHO DO REGULAR
PHYSICAL ACTIVITY HAVE UP TO A 35% LOWER RISK OF
CORONARY HEART DISEASE AND STROKE

CHALLENGE TOMORROW:

BEAT YOUR PREVIOUS RECORD FOR
STAR JUMPS

Three things I am thankful for today are:

1. --

2. --

3. --

Today I am proud of myself for:

My favourite moment of today was:

Tomorrow I am looking forward to:

Before the day comes to an end I wish to have achieved:

1. --

2. --

3. --

CONTEMPLATE TODAY:

NEVER, EVER UNDERESTIMATE THE IMPORTANCE OF HAVING FUN – RANDY PAUSCH

CHALLENGE TOMORROW:

THINK OF SOMETHING THAT YOU WOULD NORMALLY TAKE SERIOUSLY, HAVE FUN WITH IT INSTEAD

Three things I am thankful for today are:

1. --

2. --

3. --

Today I am proud of myself for:

My favourite moment of today was:

Tomorrow I am looking forward to:

DATE . ./. ./. .

Before the day comes to an end I wish to have achieved:

1. --

2. --

3. --

CONTEMPLATE TODAY:

WHAT CAN YOU DO TO HELP CREATE THE WORLD THAT YOU WOULD LIKE TO LIVE IN?

CHALLENGE TOMORROW:

ANSWER THE ABOVE HERE:

Three things I am thankful for today are:

1. --

2. --

3. --

Today I am proud of myself for:

My favourite moment of today was:

Tomorrow I am looking forward to:

Before the day comes to an end I wish to have achieved:

1. ---

2. ---

3. ---

CONTEMPLATE TODAY:

MINDFULNESS CAN BOOST ATTENTION/CONCENTRATION

CHALLENGE TOMORROW:

DO TWO 15-MINUTE MINDFULNESS OF THE BREATH MEDITATIONS

Three things I am thankful for today are:

1. ---

2. ---

3. ---

Today I am proud of myself for:

My favourite moment of today was:

Tomorrow I am looking forward to:

DATE . ./. ./. .

Before the day comes to an end I wish to have achieved:

1. ------

2. ------

3. ------

CONTEMPLATE TODAY:

YOU CAN ALWAYS TEACH THE BRAIN MORE

CHALLENGE TOMORROW:

THINK OF SOMETHING YOU HAVE ALWAYS WANTED TO LEARN, BOOK A LESSON

Three things I am thankful for today are:

1. ------

2. ------

3. ------

Today I am proud of myself for:

My favourite moment of today was:

Tomorrow I am looking forward to:

Before the day comes to an end I wish to have achieved:

1. --

2. --

3. --

CONTEMPLATE TODAY:

HUMANS ARE THE ONLY SPECIES KNOWN TO BLUSH

CHALLENGE TOMORROW:
GIVE SOMEONE A COMPLIMENT WHO
YOU WOULD NOT USUALLY

Three things I am thankful for today are:

1. --

2. --

3. --

Today I am proud of myself for:

My favourite moment of today was:

Tomorrow I am looking forward to:

DATE . ./. ./. .

Before the day comes to an end I wish to have achieved:

1. ....

2. ....

3. ....

CONTEMPLATE TODAY:

IT IS EXERCISE ALONE THAT SUPPORTS THE SPIRITS, AND
KEEPS THE MIND IN VIGOUR— MARCUS TULLIUS CICERO

CHALLENGE TOMORROW:
DO 30 MINUTES OF EXERCISE KNOWING THE
BENEFITS YOU WILL EXPERIENCE

Three things I am thankful for today are:

1. ....

2. ....

3. ....

Today I am proud of myself for:

....

My favourite moment of today was:

....

Tomorrow I am looking forward to:

....

Before the day comes to an end I wish to have achieved:

1. --

2. --

3. --

CONTEMPLATE TODAY:

IT IS KIND OF FUN TO DO THE IMPOSSIBLE
– WALT DISNEY

CHALLENGE TOMORROW:

WRITE A PLAN OF HOW YOU CAN MAKE A PATH TO YOUR IMPOSSIBLE GOAL IDENTIFIED PREVIOUSLY

Three things I am thankful for today are:

1. --

2. --

3. --

Today I am proud of myself for:

My favourite moment of today was:

Tomorrow I am looking forward to:

DATE . ./. ./. .

Before the day comes to an end I wish to have achieved:

1. --

2. --

3. --

CONTEMPLATE TODAY:

FRIENDS AND GOOD MANNERS WILL CARRY YOU WHERE
MONEY WILL NOT GO — MARGARET WALKER

CHALLENGE TOMORROW:

BE POLITE TO EVERYONE,
ESPECIALLY IF THEY ARE NOT TO YOU

Three things I am thankful for today are:

1. --

2. --

3. --

Today I am proud of myself for:

My favourite moment of today was:

Tomorrow I am looking forward to:

Before the day comes to an end I wish to have achieved:

1. ....

2. ....

3. ....

Three things I am thankful for today are:

1. ....

2. ....

3. ....

Today I am proud of myself for:

....

My favourite moment of today was:

....

Tomorrow I am looking forward to:

....

DATE . ./. ./. .

Before the day comes to an end I wish to have achieved:

1. ---

2. ---

3. ---

CONTEMPLATE TODAY:

WE CAN ONLY LEARN TO LOVE BY LOVING
– IRIS MURDOCH

CHALLENGE TOMORROW:
THINK OF SOMEONE YOU FIND IT HARD TO HAVE WARM FEELINGS TOWARDS AND OPEN YOUR HEART TO THEM

Three things I am thankful for today are:

1. ---

2. ---

3. ---

Today I am proud of myself for:

My favourite moment of today was:

Tomorrow I am looking forward to:

Before the day comes to an end I wish to have achieved:

1. --

2. --

3. --

CONTEMPLATE TODAY:

WHERE THERE IS A WILL, THERE IS A WAY
– PAULINE KAEL

CHALLENGE TOMORROW:
THINK OF SOMETHING YOU WOULD LOVE TO
DO FOR SOMEONE, MAKE IT HAPPEN

Three things I am thankful for today are:

1. --

2. --

3. --

Today I am proud of myself for:

My favourite moment of today was:

Tomorrow I am looking forward to:

DATE . ./. ./. .

Before the day comes to an end I wish to have achieved:

1. --

2. --

3. --

CONTEMPLATE TODAY:
IT IS MEDICALLY PROVEN THAT PEOPLE WHO DO REGULAR PHYSICAL ACTIVITY HAVE UP TO A 30% LOWER RISK OF DEPRESSION
CHALLENGE TOMORROW:
BEAT YOUR PREVIOUS RECORD FOR SQUATS

Three things I am thankful for today are:

1. --

2. --

3. --

Today I am proud of myself for:

My favourite moment of today was:

Tomorrow I am looking forward to:

Before the day comes to an end I wish to have achieved:

1. --

2. --

3. --

CONTEMPLATE TODAY:

IF YOU COULD GRANT ONE WISH FOR YOURSELF
WHAT WOULD IT BE?

CHALLENGE TOMORROW:
WRITE YOUR ANSWER TO THE ABOVE HERE AND
HOW YOU CAN MAKE IT COME TRUE:

Three things I am thankful for today are:

1. --

2. --

3. --

Today I am proud of myself for:

My favourite moment of today was:

Tomorrow I am looking forward to:

DATE . ./. ./. .

Before the day comes to an end I wish to have achieved:

1. ---

2. ---

3. ---

CONTEMPLATE TODAY:

WHO DO YOU THINK YOU ARE?

CHALLENGE TOMORROW:
VISIT WWW.TED.COM AND WATCH THANDIE NEWTON'S
TALK ON EMBRACING OTHERNESS

Three things I am thankful for today are:

1. ---

2. ---

3. ---

Today I am proud of myself for:

My favourite moment of today was:

Tomorrow I am looking forward to:

Before the day comes to an end I wish to have achieved:

1. --

2. --

3. --

CONTEMPLATE TODAY:

MEDITATION IS THE TONGUE OF THE SOUL AND THE LANGUAGE OF OUR SPIRIT – JEREMY TAYLOR

CHALLENGE TOMORROW:

DO A 20-MINUTE LOVING-KINDNESS MEDITATION

Three things I am thankful for today are:

1. --

2. --

3. --

Today I am proud of myself for:

My favourite moment of today was:

Tomorrow I am looking forward to:

DATE . ./. ./. .

Before the day comes to an end I wish to have achieved:

1. --

2. --

3. --

CONTEMPLATE TODAY:

ANY NEGATIVE CAN ALSO BE A POSITIVE

CHALLENGE TOMORROW:

TAKE WHAT COULD BE THOUGHT OF AS A BAD PART
OF THE DAY AND TURN IT AROUND

Three things I am thankful for today are:

1. --

2. --

3. --

Today I am proud of myself for:

My favourite moment of today was:

Tomorrow I am looking forward to:

Before the day comes to an end I wish to have achieved:

1. --

2. --

3. --

CONTEMPLATE TODAY:
IT TAKES GENEROSITY TO DISCOVER THE WHOLE THROUGH OTHERS.
IF YOU REALISE YOU ARE ONLY A VIOLIN, YOU CAN OPEN YOURSELF TO THE WORLD
BY PLAYING YOUR ROLE IN THE CONCERT – JACQUES YVES COUSTEAU
CHALLENGE TOMORROW:
VISIT WWW.THANKYOU.CO AND READ THEIR STORY, WHAT
PART COULD YOU ACT ON EARTH'S STAGE?

Three things I am thankful for today are:

1. --

2. --

3. --

Today I am proud of myself for:

My favourite moment of today was:

Tomorrow I am looking forward to:

DATE . ./. ./. .

Before the day comes to an end I wish to have achieved:

1. --

2. --

3. --

CONTEMPLATE TODAY:

IF EXERCISE WERE A PILL, IT WOULD BE ONE OF THE MOST
COST-EFFECTIVE DRUGS EVER INVENTED – DR NICK CAVILL

CHALLENGE TOMORROW:

FIND A RACE/EVENT YOU WOULD LIKE TO
COMPLETE, BOOK IT

Three things I am thankful for today are:

1. --

2. --

3. --

Today I am proud of myself for:

My favourite moment of today was:

Tomorrow I am looking forward to:

Before the day comes to an end I wish to have achieved:

1. --

2. --

3. --

CONTEMPLATE TODAY:

ONCE YOU CAN ACCEPT FAILURE, YOU CAN HAVE FUN
AND SUCCESS – RICKEY HENDERSON

CHALLENGE TOMORROW:

FORGIVE YOURSELF FOR YOUR MISTAKES

Three things I am thankful for today are:

1. --

2. --

3. --

Today I am proud of myself for:

My favourite moment of today was:

Tomorrow I am looking forward to:

DATE . ./. ./. .

Before the day comes to an end I wish to have achieved:

1. --

2. --

3. --

CONTEMPLATE TODAY:
YOU CAN MAKE MORE FRIENDS IN TWO MONTHS BY BECOMING
INTERESTED IN OTHER PEOPLE THAN YOU CAN IN TWO YEARS BY TRYING TO
GET OTHER PEOPLE INTERESTED IN YOU — DALE CARNEGIE

CHALLENGE TOMORROW:
ASK THREE PEOPLE A QUESTION THAT YOU DO
NOT KNOW ABOUT THEM

Three things I am thankful for today are:

1. --

2. --

3. --

Today I am proud of myself for:

My favourite moment of today was:

Tomorrow I am looking forward to:

Before the day comes to an end I wish to have achieved:

1. --

2. --

3. --

CONTEMPLATE TODAY:

MINDFULNESS CAN IMPROVE RELATIONSHIPS

CHALLENGE TOMORROW:

GO FOR A 30-MINUTE MINDFUL WALK

Three things I am thankful for today are:

1. --

2. --

3. --

Today I am proud of myself for:

My favourite moment of today was:

Tomorrow I am looking forward to:

DATE . ./. ./. .

Before the day comes to an end I wish to have achieved:

1. --

2. --

3. --

CONTEMPLATE TODAY:

RESENTMENT IS LIKE DRINKING POISON AND WAITING FOR THE OTHER PERSON TO DIE – CARRIE FISHER

CHALLENGE TOMORROW:

FORGIVE

Three things I am thankful for today are:

1. --

2. --

3. --

Today I am proud of myself for:

My favourite moment of today was:

Tomorrow I am looking forward to:

You Did It!

There you have it, you are now officially a 180 day challenge champion. I am so proud that you made it all the way and I really hope you enjoyed your journey. For now there is just one last reflection, how has this diary affected your life?

REFLECTION

Thank You!

From the bottom of my heart, thank you for sharing my dream to make the world a happier place. If you feel that this has been a worthwhile experience then please do spread the word to anyone you think it could help. I truly wish you all the best and I hope that you have all the courage you need to continue the good habits you have created. Your new way of life has only just begun.